Tech 2.0

World-Changing Entertainment Companies

Netflix, Amazon, Hulu, and Streaming Video

by Michael Burgan

ESports: A Billion Eyeballs and Growing

GoPro®, Garmin®, and Camera Drones

Netflix®, Amazon®, Hulu®, and Streaming Video

Pixar®, Disney®, DreamWorks®, and Digital Animation

Spotify®, Pandora®, and Streaming Music

YouTube® and Videos of Everything!

Tech **2.0** World-Changing Entertainment Companies

Netflix®, Amazon®, Hulu®, and Streaming Video

by Michael Burgan

Mason Crest

Mason Crest
450 Parkway Drive, Suite D
Broomall, PA 19008
www.masoncrest.com

© 2019 by Mason Crest, an imprint of National Highlights, Inc.

Printed and bound in the United States of America.

Series ISBN: 978-1-4222-4053-3
Hardback ISBN: 978-1-4222-4056-4
EBook ISBN: 978-1-4222-7736-2

First printing
1 3 5 7 9 8 6 4 2

Produced by Shoreline Publishing Group LLC
Santa Barbara, California
Editorial Director: James Buckley Jr.
Designer: Patty Kelley
www.shorelinepublishing.com
Cover photograph by Kaspar Grinvalds/Dreamstime.com

Library of Congress Cataloging-in-Publication Data
Names: Burgan, Michael, author. Title: Netflix, Amazon, Hulu, and streaming video / by Michael Burgan.
Description: Broomall, PA : Mason Crest, [2018] | Series: Tech 2.0: world changing-entertainment companies | Includes index.
Identifiers: LCCN 2017058187| ISBN 9781422240564 (hardback) | ISBN 9781422240533 (series) | ISBN 9781422277362 (ebook) Subjects: LCSH: Video rental services--Juvenile literature. | Streaming video--Juvenile literature. | Video recordings industry--Juvenile literature. | Broadcasting--Juvenile literature.
Classification: LCC HD9697.V542 B87 2018 | DDC 384.5506/5--dc23 LC record available at https://lccn.loc.gov/2017058187

QR Codes disclaimer:

CONTENTS

Introduction 6

Chapter 1: Entertainment over the Internet .10

Chapter 2: Here Comes the Competition 20

Chapter 3: A New Giant .32

Chapter 4: What's Ahead 48

Find Out More 62

Series Glossary of Key Terms. 63

Index 64

KEY ICONS TO LOOK FOR

Words to Understand: These words with their easy-to-understand definitions will increase the reader's understanding of the text, while building vocabulary skills.

Sidebars: This boxed material within the main text allows readers to build knowledge, gain insights, explore possibilities, and broaden their perspectives by weaving together additional information to provide realistic and holistic perspectives.

Educational Videos: Readers can view videos by scanning our QR codes, providing them with additional educational content to supplement the text. Examples include news coverage, moments in history, speeches, iconic moments, and much more!

Text-Dependent Questions: These questions send the reader back to the text for more careful attention to the evidence presented here.

Research Projects: Readers are pointed toward areas of further inquiry connected to each chapter. Suggestions are provided for projects that encourage deeper research and analysis.

Series Glossary of Key Terms: This back-of-the-book glossary contains terminology used throughout this series. Words found here increase the reader's ability to read and comprehend higher-level books and articles in this field.

Tech 2.0 Introduction

Pulling out a smartphone or tablet computer and watching a favorite TV show or movie is a part of life for millions of people around the world. Today's streaming video services give consumers the ability to watch content almost anywhere and any time they want. And the desire for greater freedom and choice has led a number of companies to enter the business of providing access to that content. The companies present old programming as well as create new shows and movies just for their customers.

The technology that makes streaming video possible has been around for less than 30 years. At the heart of the technology is the internet, which since the 1970s has helped people use their computers to share information around the world. But it took many developments to go from sending emails or small amounts of data through the network to be able to stream videos. The development of the World Wide Web made it easier for people not familiar with computers to access the internet. Then internet providers began to increase the bandwidth of their systems—the amount of data that can be sent at any one time and how fast it travels. Data sent over the internet is measured in electrical signals called bits, and the speed at which the information travels is measured in millions of bits per second (mbps).

Before the rise of the World Wide Web in the 1990s, most people accessed the internet over a telephone line. The speed of the data was then measured in thousands of bits per second. The use of cable TV systems to transmit data enabled the greater speeds common today—and opened the door to streaming video.

Improvements in cell phone technology and the ability to send computer data wirelessly also shaped the streaming video revolution. With an app on their phone, people can watch the same movies that were once only available in the theaters or on TV.

But making streaming video a common part of daily life took more than technology. It took companies that took a chance on the new technology. They believed they could make money by giving people more choices over what to watch and when to watch it. One company took the lead in making streaming video a reality—Netflix. With its success, other companies have entered the field, with Amazon and Hulu among the best known. Having several companies in the streaming video field means people can choose the service that's just right for them, based on price and the content available. And the demand for new programming, not just repeats of old movies and TV shows, has opened up great opportunities for many creative people. The video

Sure, a movie theater is still fun . . . but with streaming, you stay home!

streaming companies hire writers, directors, and actors to make shows that might never have appeared on a traditional TV network or at a movie theater.

Streaming video has become an important tool for both entertaining and educating hundreds of millions of people. Here's a closer look at how the industry behind it developed, where it is today, and what could happen in the future.

1 Entertainment over the Internet

With the growth of the internet and increased bandwidth, companies saw that they could offer entertainment to consumers through their computers. In the early 1990s, consumers could download some entertainment onto their computers. But they couldn't watch live sporting or music events as they happened, and their choices were limited. Watching movies at home still meant going to the video store to buy or rent a videotape. People had been watching movies that way since the 1970s. Some videodiscs were available, but few people had the players. In 1995, several companies introduced a new disc format, the digital videodisc (DVD), but it would take several years for it to become popular.

Even before the introduction of the DVD, computer engineers were trying to perfect the streaming of video and music. This would let

WORDS TO UNDERSTAND

algorithm a set of steps a computer program follows to solve a problem or perform a certain task

broadband the fastest internet connection available to most homes, usually offered through a cable TV service

compress shrink in size

decompress return something that has been compressed to its original size

download take information on the internet and store it on a computer

consumers access the content without first **downloading** it to their computers. The first events streamed were live concerts, in 1994. The next year, the sports network ESPN streamed radio coverage of a baseball game. Streaming audio was easier, because it took less bandwidth. The technology of the day limited the picture quality of video streams.

Through the 1990s, Microsoft, a major software company, worked on improving streaming video. Sometimes they did this by buying small companies that had developed useful technology. But Microsoft had competition. In 1997, RealNetworks offered consumers access to hundreds of radio stations over the internet, and its software could stream some video too. But through the 1990s, picture

RealNetworks was the first streaming site to break out.

A Leader with Vision

When Reed Hastings began his business career, vacuum cleaners, not video, were his focus. For a time, he sold the cleaners going door-to-door, showing potential customers how well his product worked. After studying mathematics in college, Hastings took a job at a company that tried to improve computer software. He started his first company, Pure Software, in 1991, and it did the same kind of work. Pure Software grew quickly and in 1996 merged with another software company. The next year, the new company was sold, and Hastings decided to do something new. With money he made from the sale of his company, he and Marc Randolph started Netflix. (Randolph left the company five years later.) According to one story, the partners did a test mailing of an audio CD to make sure the disc would arrive undamaged. When that worked, they began their DVD business. The success of Netflix has made Hastings a billionaire. When he's not running the company, he spends some of his time trying to help poor students go to college and study science, technology, engineering, and mathematics.

quality remained poor, and the video image could not fill an entire computer stream.

While efforts at improving streaming technology went on, changes were happening in how consumers could watch movies. In 1997, Reed Hastings founded the company Netflix. His idea was to let consumers use their computers to choose the DVDs they wanted, then receive the discs in the mail. By only using DVDs, Hastings saved money, since they were cheaper to mail than videotapes. He also assumed that in time, more people would switch to DVDs because they were easier to use and had better picture quality than tapes.

Rental Revolution

Starting in 1998, Netflix customers began renting discs. People could buy them as well, but Hastings soon stopped selling the discs to focus on renting them. He made other changes, too. In 1999, he introduced a subscription plan with no late fees. Most video stores, and Netflix too, usually charged the fees when customers didn't return their rentals on time. Now, though, Netflix customers could keep discs as long as they wanted, but they could only have up to four discs at one time. When they sent one disc back to Netflix, they received the next one on their list of choices. By 2000, almost all customers were on the subscription plan, and Netflix soon stopped renting discs one at a time.

As the company grew, Netflix offered more features. One was giving suggestions of movies people might like to watch, based on the movies they had already seen. The computer program that made these suggestions used what's called an **algorithm**. The program also looked at the viewing habits of other people with similar tastes

These red envelopes were familiar sights in the early 2000s.

to any one consumer. That also helped the program make suggestions for what people might like.

By 2002, Netflix had 500,000 users, but the company was not making money. To ensure customers got their discs quickly, Netflix opened warehouses across the United States, which took a lot of money to build. But Netflix had an advantage over video stores. It offered tens of thousands of movies—many more than any one store could. Its membership continued to grow, reaching more than four million by 2005. By then, the video store company Blockbuster was offering its own video-by-mail service. But it entered the field too late to catch Netflix.

With ongoing improvements in streaming internet technology, Hastings had a new idea. He would offer movies to consumers directly through their computer, with no discs involved. Customers could watch what they wanted when they wanted, still paying just the monthly subscription fee. The new service began in 2007. The new streaming technology improvements included better ways to **compress** the digital content, and then **decompress** it at the user's computer. The process made large files smaller, which meant they could be sent faster over the internet without a loss of quality. Netflix also had good timing, because by 2007, about half of all American homes had a **broadband** connection that provided the bandwidth needed to stream movies with good quality.

The speed of broadband made streaming videos possible . . . and fast.

Here Comes Streaming

When Netflix introduced its streaming service, the idea of "on demand" video wasn't new. During the 1990s, several communications companies tried to create on-demand systems, sending out the movies over phone lines or the cables used for cable TV. By 2007, cable TV companies were offering on-demand movies, charging customers for each movie they wanted. But once again, Netflix had

An Early Test of On-Demand Video

While Reed Hastings was just planning Netflix, a company in Hong Kong (right) was already developing an on-demand TV service. The service, called iTV, launched in March 1998. Using a box that connected to their TVs, customers could access movies, recorded music, and radio through a phone line. With movies, customers could use their remote to pause the scene, just as they could with videotape or DVD players. After one year of service, iTV had about 80,000 customers. But it also had some problems. Because of legal arrangements between iTV and movie studios, a limited number of people could watch the same movie at once. One customer reported he had to wait 45 minutes to start one particularly popular movie. It took more than $1 billion to launch iTV, but the company failed soon after it began. On-demand video that worked well was still to come.

some advantages. It had a larger library of movies, and customers could watch as many movies as they wanted every month for just one low fee. Streaming was also a plus for Netflix. It cut its mailing costs, and the company didn't need to keep as many discs in its warehouses.

Not all the programming in the Netflix library was available to stream. Many people continued watching movies on DVDs that came in the mail. But Hastings believed that streaming was the way of the future. He said, "Over time, all video around the world is going to become internet video where each person can choose what they want to watch." As more TV shows became available, Netflix users could also binge-watch—they could watch many episodes of a specific show in one evening.

Offering both streaming video and disc rentals, Netflix kept growing. In 2010 it began offering its services outside the United

An early Netflix ad

States, starting in Canada. That year, it had 20 million subscribers. Not all of them streamed, but other companies realized that they could make money offering their own streaming service. Even as Netflix was rolling out its streaming service in 2007, two other companies had a similar idea.

Text-Dependent Questions

1. Along with Microsoft, what other company was one of the first to offer streaming content over the internet?

2. Why was getting customers to stream movies rather than rent DVDs a benefit for Netflix?

3. How did compressing and then decompressing data help Netflix?

Research Project

Several websites can perform tests to check the speed of an internet connection. Find one and test the speed of the connection of all the computers in your home or several at school. What is the fastest speed? Do some devices have faster speeds than others?

2 Here Comes the Competition

W hile Netflix was taking control of the DVD market and making plans to stream content, several large television companies became worried. They saw clips of some of their shows running on YouTube. Millions of people watched the clips, which was good, but the companies didn't receive any money for the views, which the companies didn't like.

Leaders at two major TV networks decided they wanted to get in on the growing trend to stream videos on the internet. In 2006, Fox and NBCUniversal joined forces to create Hulu. The service launched in 2007 and offered viewers programs from those two TV networks that had already been **broadcast**. People could see a show they might have missed or watch a favorite one over and over. The service was free, but customers had to watch ads to see the content.

WORDS TO UNDERSTAND

broadcast a radio or TV show available to many people at once, with the signal to receive the program sent through the air or a cable; also, the act of sending out that signal

queue a list of programming that someone wants to watch

venture capitalists people who invest money in new companies, expecting to make more money in the future

The driving force behind shaping Hulu was Jason Kilar. After working at the online giant Amazon for ten years, Kilar was hired to get Hulu off the ground and make it a success. He sometimes had trouble getting what he wanted, such as certain shows from the networks' libraries. His company did not have to pay the networks for the shows, and the people at Fox and NBC who created the shows didn't like that arrangement. But the top officials at the TV companies wanted Hulu to succeed, so Kilar convinced Fox and NBC to accept most of his ideas. These included having fewer commercials than would be shown on a regular broadcast of a TV show. And if consumers didn't like a particular commercial, they could choose another. From his time at Amazon, Kilar learned how important it was to keep custom-

Broadcast networks like NBC had to adjust their business to streaming.

A Newcomer to Television

Growing up, Jason Kilar (pictured) became fascinated with Walt Disney, the man who made some of the best-loved animated films of all time. Disney also knew something about technology, which he used to make Disneyland, Disney World, and Epcot popular vacation destinations. Kilar worked for a time for the Disney Company, and that helped fuel his desire to give customers what they want. Making customers happy was also a message he learned while working at Amazon. Kilar spent ten years there before taking over at Hulu in 2007. He often worked directly with Amazon founder Jeff Bezos. Thanks to his Amazon experience, Kilar stressed making Hulu as easy to use as possible. He learned a lot about internet  technology while working there, but he had no experience with television programming. That sometimes led to his conflicts with the leaders of some officials at the TV networks. Kilar left Hulu in 2013 and started a new online video service called Vessel, which he sold in 2016.

ers happy. Hulu also added a social element to viewing, as customers could post comments about a show or easily share clips of an episode on other websites. Like Netflix, Hulu also added a **queue**, so viewers could easily keep track of shows they wanted to watch in the future.

Money Talk

Hulu also offered help to companies that bought ads on the service. When users first signed up, they submitted information about themselves, such as their age or whether or not they had children. That way, companies could target their ads to viewers most likely to buy their products. Kilar said in a 2009 interview in *Fast Company*, "I have a big belief that if you don't have children under the age of two, you don't need to see a [diapers] commercial."

Within two years of its launch, Hulu offered whole episodes or clips from 800 different shows. It also had more than 400 movies in its video library. About 38 million people were watching the service at some time. The company was earning about $120 million as companies bought time to show their ads. Also in 2009, Disney, owner of the ABC network, joined the Hulu project.

Around the same time as Hulu gained access to the ABC shows, the networks that owned the streaming service wanted to make more money. The way to do that, they decided, was to offer a second set of programming. Hulu Plus came on the air in 2010. For $7.99 per month, customers could watch more shows, see new episodes sooner after they were first broadcast, and see fewer commercials. Hulu

TV host Jimmy Kimmel was an early adopter of streaming.

Cutting the Cable Cord

Streaming video must be watched on a device connected to the internet. But as Netflix, Hulu, and other companies began their streaming services, most TVs were not able to connect directly to the internet. Several companies stepped in to offer devices that would receive an internet signal and deliver it to a television. The first was Roku, which actually began as a part of Netflix. At first, Netflix was the only streaming

service available on the device. But over time, Roku was able to stream content from other companies, and the company offered different versions of the box at different prices. It cost more to stream shows with the highest picture quality of 1080p. The "p" stands for progressive scan and 1080 is number of lines of digital data a screen can display. 720p and 1080p are both considered high-definition (HD) television. With the success of streaming video, other companies now offer devices that compete with Roku, including Amazon and Apple. The ease of using these devices on both TVs and computers, and the amount of content available, has led several million Americans to get rid of their cable TV subscriptions. This is often called "cutting the cord," and experts expect more people to do it in the years to come.

Plus would also be available on more devices that streamed video. In 2011, after introducing the new service, Hulu earned more than $400 million.

Setting the price for Hulu Plus was not easy. As he had in the past, Kilar sometimes argued with Hulu's owners. The networks thought their shows were worth more money than Kilar wanted to charge. And Hulu was still a small part of their business. The networks made more money selling ads when the shows first aired on regular TV and by charging cable companies to carry the shows.

Hulu offers live TV, movies, TV shows, and original programming.

But the networks knew that they gained viewers by streaming content. And with Netflix growing its streaming service, Kilar insisted on the $7.99 price so Hulu could match its competitor. Hulu later charged $11.99 for a service with no ads, and it eventually stopped offering a free service.

Vudu and Apple Join the Fun

As ABC, NBC, and Fox built Hulu, another company started its own streaming service. In 2005, a company called Vudu started working on a device that would stream movies to a TV. It would take until 2007, though, for Vudu to finally offer its service to consumers.

Former Apple exec Alain Rossmann helped build Vudu.

The founders of Vudu were Alain Rossmann and Tony Maranz. Rossmann had worked for Apple during the 1980s, helping the company design computers. He then started several of his own companies in a part of California known as Silicon Valley, where many small tech firms got their start. Some of them eventually became hugely successful, including Apple and Google. Maranz also had a background in computer technology. He was frustrated with not being able to rent old movies at his local video store. And waiting for discs to come through the mail from Netflix was too slow. He convinced Rossmann to work with him to create a service that would connect a box to a TV and stream movies. At the time, consumers could download some movies onto their computers, but the downloading took a lot of time. Plus, many people wanted to watch the movies on a larger TV screen.

To get Vudu running, Rossmann and Maranz did what many Silicon Valley companies did, and still do. They sought money from companies called **venture capitalists**. Two venture capitalist companies agreed to fund Vudu. Then, as the company's engineers designed the box that would bring the movies to a television, Maranz made deals with almost every major studio to show some of their films.

Vudu began in 2007 with a library of 5,000 movies. The first 30 seconds of each movie was stored in the box, which had a hard drive just like a computer has to store information. Those stored segments meant the movies began as soon as someone pressed play. Then, the rest of the movie streamed through the internet and into the box as the viewer watched. Consumers bought the box that connected to their TV for $400. After that, they paid for each movie

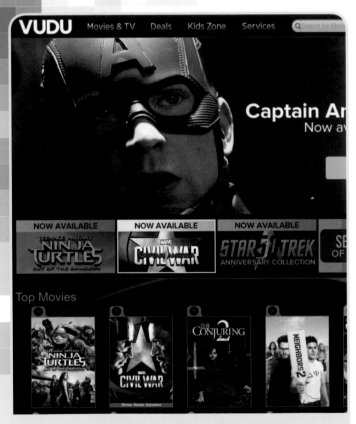

Vudu's home screen pointed fans to favorites.

they watched. The picture quality was as good as with a DVD, and users could go backward and forward in a movie as it played, as they could with a DVD. As Vudu prepared to launch, Maranz told *The New York Times*, "Other forms of movie distribution are going to look silly and uncompetitive by comparison." Despite that claim, most people did not rush to buy a Vudu box. Vudu faced competition from Netflix, Hulu, and other companies that later entered the streaming video field. None of them required customers to buy a fairly expensive box to watch video. By 2009, Vudu had cut half its staff, leaving about 50 employees. Like many new tech companies, it was losing money, and there was no sign that it would gain customers. It lowered the price of its boxes and began working on software that would let consumers use the service through other devices, such as TVs with direct access to the internet. Eventually, it got rid of the boxes all together.

News brief on the Vudu box

Despite its problems, one company saw some value in Vudu. In 2010, the retail giant Walmart bought Vudu. Walmart already sold more DVDs than any other US company, but it saw that streaming video was the wave of the future. Buying Vudu let it enter that market. It thought that its experience selling goods to consumers would let it grow Vudu's business.

Another major US company had already entered the streaming video market. The same year Hulu and Vudu launched, Apple offered its first Apple TV device. It let users either stream content through the Apple iTunes store or download content from a computer. The iTunes store had already let consumers stream content to their

The Apple TV device offered new streaming possibilities to users.

computers, either as rentals or purchases. Some people complained, however, that the range of movies on iTunes was small and the cost was high, compared to buying DVDs at a store. A second version of Apple TV also let users stream from services such as Netflix. They could also rent TV shows.

Apple continued to make improvements to its TV system, and by 2013 the device had sales of $1 billion for the year. By then, though, Apple, Netflix, and the other streaming services were facing competition from a powerful internet company.

Text-Dependent Questions

1. What was one of the ideas Jason Kilar learned at both Disney and Amazon that he tried to apply at Hulu?

2. How did Hulu help companies target their ads to specific customers?

3. How did Vudu try to compete with other streaming services when it could not sell many of its boxes?

Research Project

Using news stories you find on the internet, identify someone who currently has an important position at Hulu or Vudu. What does this person do? Try to find out what he or she did before joining the company.

3 A New Giant

Two years before Netflix was launched, Jeff Bezos was working out of a Seattle garage and thinking about how to sell things on the internet. Bezos had a background in computers, and he decided he could shake up **e-commerce** by selling books online. He would offer low prices, a large selection, and great customer service. In 1995, his company Amazon.com went live. Within ten years, Amazon was selling a wide range of products besides books and had annual sales of more than $8 billion.

Some of the products Amazon sold were videos of movies and TV shows. By 2006, the company saw that more people were watching video content by downloading it on their computers. That year, Amazon introduced what it called Unbox, a software program that let people watch videos they bought or rented from Amazon. Consumers paid $1.99 to buy an episode of a TV show and up to $15 to buy a movie. Rentals were under $3. Viewers could watch their

WORDS TO UNDERSTAND

bundle the variety of TV channels available from a cable or streaming video company

e-commerce the buying and selling of goods over the internet

feedback good and bad comments people provide on a product or service

content on a computer, television, or mobile device.

Within two years, Amazon changed the name of the service to Amazon Video on Demand. By that point, Netflix had launched its streaming video service with its popular subscription plan. For a flat flee, customers could watch as much content as they wanted every month. Amazon, though, continued to offer its content only for purchase or rent. And downloading a movie meant there was a delay between when the customer bought it and when it actually was ready to play on their computer. In the early days of Unbox, that delay was up to ten minutes. Unbox also drew some complaints from people who owned Apple products. Amazon's video service was not available to them.

The XBox can also stream video.

Making the Switch

In 2011, more than half of Netflix's 20 million customers watched more streamed videos than rental discs. The number of devices that people could use to watch streamed video had increased. Video game devices such as Xbox and Playstation also had streaming capabilities, along with smartphones and TVs and DVD players that had internet access. Seeing Netflix's success with streaming video, Amazon introduced a new video service. Some Amazon customers were already paying a yearly fee to receive free two-day shipping on

Amazon chief Jeff Bezos has become the world's richest person.

orders worth more than $25. This service was called Amazon Prime. In 2011, the company gave Prime members free access to Amazon Prime Instant Video. Through that service, Prime members could stream about 5,000 movies and television shows, though some content did require an extra fee.

Amazon Prime Instant Video, unlike Unbox, worked on both Apple devices and PCs. It also streamed through Roku and other devices with direct internet access. But at the start, Amazon could not match the number of titles Netflix offered for streaming. And customers had to buy a yearly Amazon Prime membership to have access to the free videos—not something everyone wanted to do.

Over the next few years, however, the number of people signing up for Amazon Prime rose dramatically. Company officials believed that the appeal of their streaming service helped boost that number. While Netflix remained the king of streaming video, Amazon became its most powerful challenger. And it had one advantage over Netflix. Since Amazon Prime Instant Video was part of a much larger company, it didn't have to worry about making a profit. Netflix had to make money on its streaming to survive.

Content Creators

In their competition with each other and with major TV networks, both Amazon and Netflix began to develop their own content for streaming. Even before starting Amazon Prime, Amazon had launched

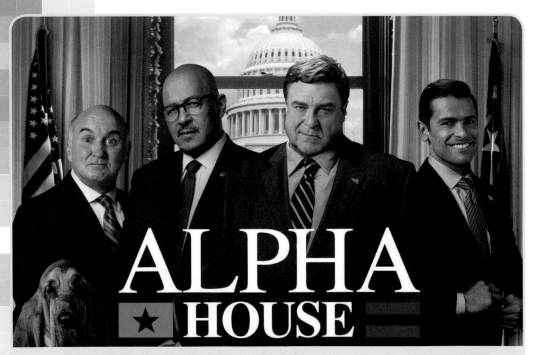

Amazon paid for production of this Washington DC-based comedy.

its own studio to make movies. By 2012, Amazon Studios had more than 30 movies and TV shows in development. And just as Amazon users could provide **feedback** on books the company sold, they played a role in deciding what movies and shows were made. Filmmakers submitted their ideas to Amazon, and both regular customers and users of the Instant Video streaming service could offer comments. Amazon also kept track of what its customers enjoyed watching online. That feedback also shaped the kind of programming Amazon Studios tried.

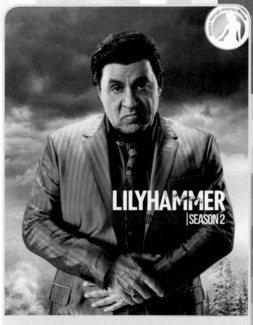

Musician Steven Van Zandt was in this series set in Norway.

In 2013, Amazon offered its first made-for-streaming TV show. *Alpha House* looked at the personal and professional lives of four U.S. senators in Washington DC. It was created by Garry Trudeau, who also created the *Doonsebury* comic strip. Trudeau had worked with other networks before. He was convinced that Amazon was serious about offering the best-quality programming possible. He also thought Amazon gave him and others great creative freedom. He said in 2014, "The experience has just been a joy and a privilege from start to finish—and I know it doesn't always unfold like that."

Netflix launched its first show just months before Amazon did. Like Amazon, Netflix relied on feedback from its customers to plan its programming. The first Netflix show, *Lilyhammer*, described the life of a former criminal who moved to Norway. Netflix followed that in 2013 with *House of Cards*. The company surprised some people in the entertainment business when it spent $100 million to produce 26 episodes of the show. No one knew if the show would be a hit. Like *Alpha House*, it also dealt with politics, but it had a serious tone. But the show featured several well-known film stars, which drew in viewers. Netflix also did something different with the show—it released all of the first season's 13 episodes at once. Binge watching now extended to new shows developed just for streaming. The term *binge-watch* was used more than ever before starting in 2014, when the second season of *House of Cards* was released. By 2015, a survey showed that two-thirds of Americans binge-watched television.

Until his harassment charge, Kevin Spacey starred in *House of Cards*.

House of Cards proved to be popular with critics and viewers alike. In its first season, members of the show's crew won three Emmy Awards, the highest honor in US television. The cast and crew won other honors for their work over the following years.

Since introducing their first original shows, Netflix and Amazon have made many more. Most are like traditional TV shows aired on broadcast TV. Each show has a certain number of episodes per season, and if a show is popular, it can last for many seasons. Both of the major streaming companies also started to make full-length movies to be shown in

Streaming for Children

While Amazon and Netflix poured billions of dollars into content for adults, they didn't ignore children and teens. This so-called family-friendly programming included both live-action and animated shows. One hit for Amazon was *Tumble Leaf*. The animated program for younger kids first aired in 2014 and won several Emmy Awards. Also from Amazon, *The Kicks* focused on a teenage soccer player adjusting to life in a new home. In 2016, Amazon bought the rights to stream much of the children's programming produced by the

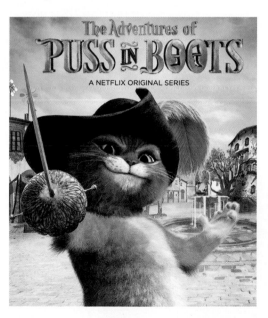

Public Broadcasting System (PBS). One Netflix offering was *The Adventures of Puss in Boots*. Puss, the feisty, sword-fighting cat from the *Shrek* movies, got his own animated series. Some of Netflix's content came from the Walt Disney Company. In 2017, Disney announced it would stop providing content to Netflix and begin its own streaming service aimed at kids and teens. Disney would offer sequels to movies originally produced for theaters, as well as TV programs. Disney made the decision as fewer people watched the Disney Channel over cable TV. A 2016 study suggested that kids, like adults, were watching less regular TV broadcasting and turning to streaming video.

both movie theaters and as streaming video. In 2015, Amazon produced *Chi-Raq* with the noted film director Spike Lee. The movie was first shown in theaters. Several months later, Amazon made the movie available to stream.

The same year, Netflix released its first feature film, *Beasts of No Nation.* It was not involved in making it; it simply bought the rights to show it. Unlike Amazon, however, Netflix released the movie to theaters at the same time it began streaming it. Netflix believed its customers should have a choice about how to see a new movie—either on the big screen in a theater or streaming on their laptop or smartphone. The owners of movie theaters did not like this approach. They wanted viewers to be able to see new films only in theaters, so they could make more money. But Netflix was committed to letting its customers see new films at home or on the go.

Netflix vs. Amazon Prime

Brad Pitt starred in the Netflix-produced film *War Machine*.

Battle of the Streamers

The competition between Netflix and Amazon continued to grow. Netflix spent millions of dollars to make movies featuring such stars as Adam Sandler and Brad Pitt. The first Sandler movie, *The Ridiculous Six*, was only available for streaming. Critics hated it, but Netflix viewers liked it enough that the company decided to make more movies with Sandler. Like *The Ridiculous Six*, they would only be available to Netflix's streaming customers.

Netflix spent at least $60 million to make *War Machine*, released in 2017, which starred Brad Pitt. The star believed Netflix and other streaming services creating new content was good for filmmakers. "There are more films, there are more stories being told...I think this is nothing but a fantastic moment for all of us." The quality of some of the movies produced by streaming companies was also on the rise. In 2017, Amazon scored a historic first. Its *Manchester by the Sea* was nominated the Academy Award for Best Film—the first time a streaming video company won that honor. Netflix also won an Academy Award that year, for its documentary *The White Helmets*.

Both Netflix and Amazon were looking to make even more feature films, while also creating new TV shows, documentaries, and comedy specials. In 2017, Netflix said it was working on releasing 40 new movies. By releasing its movies in theaters at the same time they began streaming, Netflix gave its films a chance to win major awards.

The success of Amazon's *Manchester by the Sea* was a watershed.

But it refused to delay releasing films to its streaming customers, as Amazon did. The push to make films, however, was costly for Netflix. It spent about $6 billion for its own programming in 2017. The company predicted it would take in less money than it spent for several years. Once again, Amazon Studios had an advantage. It could lose money too, but Amazon as a whole would still make a profit.

Outside the Big Two

As Netflix and Amazon battled for viewers, the other streaming companies made changes to try to compete. In 2016, Vudu introduced Movies on Us. Customers could watch movies for free, though they contained ads. Other companies had already introduced free streaming services with ads, such as Sony and Yahoo. The next year, Hulu began offering Hulu Live. Viewers could watch TV

Vudu's controller put a world of video at users' fingertips.

shows as they were first broadcast on major networks such as CBS and NBC without having cable TV. The service also included Hulu's existing library of streaming content. Other networks offered by major cable companies were also available, such as CNN, the Disney

Channel, and the Cartoon Network. The new service cost $39.95 per month.

Hulu also joined Amazon and Netflix as producers of new content. It actually aired its first original content in 2010, with the reality show *If I Can Dream.* Perhaps because fewer people watched Hulu, its shows did not always draw as much attention as shows such as *House of Cards* or Amazon's *Transparent*. But Hulu continued to increase its own productions. Its 2017 adaptation of the novel *The Handmaid's Tale* was highly popular and it won the Emmy that year for Outstanding Drama Series, along with four other awards. It was the first time a streaming company won the top honor for a drama.

Women inspired by *The Handmaid's Tale* demonstrated in Austin, Texas.

Going "Over the Top" with "Skinny Bundles"

Hulu Live joined a number of other services trying to appeal to cable TV customers seeking to "cut the cord." The networks that Hulu included in the package were commonly part of the **bundle** of channels most local cable companies provided. But those bundles of 100 channels or more often included networks customers didn't want, and at a much higher price than what Hulu Live cost. Hulu became one of a number of companies offer-

ing what were called skinny bundles. Other companies with these slimmed-down packages included Sling TV, DirectTV Now, YouTube TV, and Sony's Playstation Vue. In larger cities, some of the services also offered local TV networks. Skinny bundle buyers use what are called over-the-top devices to watch content. These include Roku, video game boxes, and any other device that connect wirelessly to the internet. Some major

networks also offer their own over-the-top programming that is not part of a bundle of channels. HBO Now and CBS All Access are two examples of cable and traditional broadcast networks entering the streaming video field.

In 2017, one of the biggest US internet companies entered the streaming video market. Facebook introduced Watch, which offered viewers short videos, programs from cable TV networks, and a limited number of Major League Baseball games. Facebook said it would spend $1 billion to show original content not available elsewhere, including reality shows and comedies. At almost the same time, Apple said it would also spend $1 billion to create original shows for Apple TV.

Streaming users can now watch live MLB action on Facebook.

Text-Dependent Questions

1. Why does Amazon Prime have to be less concerned about making a profit than Netflix?

2. Why do people like Garry Trudeau and Brad Pitt think streaming companies are good for people who make movies and TV shows?

3. What was the importance of *The Handmaid's Tale* winning an Emmy in 2017?

Research Project

Find three original shows now airing on Netflix, Amazon, and Hulu. How many seasons have they been on? Has any of them won any awards?

4 What's Ahead

Streaming video has become incredibly successful around the world. By 2017, Netflix streamed content in almost every country, and programming was available in 20 languages. Its number of international subscribers grew by 5 million in the last quarter of 2016—more than its increase in the United States. Amazon Prime had almost the same global reach, though it still trailed Netflix in total subscribers.

All the leading streaming video companies realize they must keep improving their product to keep old subscribers and attract new ones. For Netflix, that has meant, in part, hiring hundreds of engineers who try to improve the company's algorithms. The goal is to continue to give viewers more programs that match their tastes. Making a better service has also included offering even more original content. That effort includes using the newest video technology.

WORDS TO UNDERSTAND

net neutrality the idea that internet service providers should enable equal access to any content they deliver

pixels tiny dots on a TV or computer screen that form visible images

servers powerful computers that provide data to other computers

Since the 1990s, the makers of video equipment have worked to improve the quality of the images seen on TVs and other devices. The first high-definition (HD) TV sets appeared in 1998. The same year, TV networks began broadcasting their shows in HD. A TV set's picture quality is measured by lines of resolution—vertical lines of **pixels** that help create the image (there are horizontal lines too). Until 1998, a typical TV had at most 480 lines of resolution. With HD sets, the highest number of lines jumped to 1080, offering a much sharper picture. At first, though, the cost of these sets was high—up to $10,000. But as more people bought them and the technology improved, the price came down. And for people who watched broadcast TV networks, having the new sets was the only way to watch HD shows.

Over time, the manufacturers of TV sets increased the resolution of their sets. In 2013, Sony introduced the first 4K sets. The name referred to four thousand—roughly the number of horizontal pixels or vertical lines of resolution, as compared to 1920 horizontal pixels or vertical lines of resolution with the 1080 sets. 4K was also sometimes called Ultra HD.

Improving Picture Quality

Netflix and the other streaming companies had to react to these technological changes. Their customers with the new sets expected to see the best picture quality possible when they streamed. Netflix and the others began streaming their content in HD, though not all viewers saw the same picture quality. The speed of their internet connection or the browser they used could lower the quality from 1080 to 720 lines of resolution. That was still considered high definition, though obviously the quality was not as good as 1080 content. People who watched streaming video through a Roku or similar device had to make sure it could handle HD content.

In 2014, Netflix began streaming some of its content in 4K. Once again, customers needed even more bandwidth on their internet connection to see the images in 4K. Amazon and Hulu also began to offer 4K content. By 2016, the companies were also offering 4K programs with high dynamic range (HDR). With this technology, there is greater contrast between light and dark parts of an image. The higher contrast gives a sharper image. A TV with HDR and fewer lines of resolution can look better than a TV with higher resolution but no HDR.

The 4K picture quality will greatly improve video streaming.

At the same time 4K was taking off, TV makers were selling sets that could show content in 3D. The idea of watching movies in three dimensions—height, width, and depth—went back decades. People could see 3D movies in theaters starting in the 1950s, though they had to wear special glasses to get the 3D effect, which is still true today. The glasses were also required to watch the 3D TVs, which were first sold in 2010. Netflix said in 2014 that it would offer 3D content. The televisions, though, never caught on with many people. By 2017, several TV makers announced they would no longer sell 3D sets.

Here Comes VR

By then, however, other new technologies were being developed. The year before, some viewers had the first chance to watch a virtual reality (VR) broadcast of an NCAA basketball game. Turner Sports, part of Turner Broadcasting, shows different sporting events on different cable channels and also streams content for the NCAA. For the finals of the 2016 basketball championship, Turner worked with the VR company Oculus to show that game in VR.

Different companies have been working to bring virtual reality to gaming and video for several years. Oculus, owned by Facebook, has been a leader

Wearing a VR headset, viewers will have a new amazing experience.

The Battle over Bandwidth

By 2014, the popularity of streaming video was becoming an issue for the major internet service providers (ISPs). Verizon accused Netflix in particular of being a bandwidth "hog." During peak watching times in the evening, the demand for Netflix content could take up 30 percent or more of the available bandwidth—far more than for any other streaming company. Verizon wanted Netflix to pay for the cost of delivering all that content to its customers. Netflix argued that it already paid another company to bring content from its **servers** to the ISPs, like Verizon, so it shouldn't have to pay again. Netflix feared that if it had to pay more money to have adequate bandwidth, it would have to raise its fees. That could lead some customers to drop the service. In the end, Netflix signed deals with Verizon and Comcast, another major ISP. Netflix paid them directly, rather than paying the company that had been the "bridge" between Netflix and the ISPs. Netflix also battled the ISPs when they tried to limit how much data customers could access during a month. The ISPs hoped that if customers could not watch as much streaming video through the internet, they would watch more of the cable broadcasts the ISPs also sold. Netflix responded in part by finding a way to compress data and reduce the bandwidth needed to stream its content.

in the field. What the viewers of the NCAA game saw was actually 180-degree video, which is similar to VR. With real virtual reality content, viewers seem to enter a scene or worlds that aren't real. They do this by wearing a special headset, which looks like huge goggles. The same goggles can also give the experience of seeing a live sporting event in 180-degree or 360-degree. With 360-degree viewers can see the event from all angles, but they can't seem to enter the space they see, as they can with a VR video game. With the Turner Sports event in 180-degree, viewers could not see what was behind them, but they saw the full view of the action from left to right. Technology experts expect 360-degree content to become more common, followed by true VR.

This image is just a sample of what 360-degree video can show.

For now, though, 360-degree content is hard to find on the major streaming services. The content requires more bandwidth than regular content, and the best headsets needed to watch 360-degree and VR are not cheap. When Netflix released its first 360-degree video in 2016, it was just a short scene from its show

The Jump to 12K

While 4K video made streamed content sharper than before, engineers were already thinking ahead to the future. Virtual reality and 360-degree programming would require even more lines of resolution to give viewers a lifelike experience. The human eye sees the world in a resolution that is equal to what a 16K video image would provide. In 2017, a company called Visbit demonstrated its step toward reaching the goal of 16K video. It streamed a 12K 360-degree video over wifi. Visbit's technology also let viewers zoom in on a particular part of the image. The company said that in the future, the technology could let someone watching a 360-degree sporting event zoom in a particular player.

Visbit admitted, though, that it would take several years before cameras able to shoot in 12K would be commonly available.

Stranger Things. The clip, though, was shown on YouTube, not through Netflix. That year, both Netflix and Hulu had apps that let people with VR headsets watch their shows. Hulu, though, offered content that was actually 360-degree—viewers could see in all directions. When Netflix introduced its VR app, customers only saw traditional two-dimensional content through the headset. One big complaint about watching video through the headsets was that people could not do it together. In 2017, Hulu addressed that. It released a new app that let up to three people watch the same event at the same time, with each person using their own headset.

FCC chairman Ajit Pay spearheaded loosening net neutrality rules.

Net neutrality demands that ISPs shoul

Net neutrality explained

Other Future Challenges

Adapting to new technologies quickly is just one issue for streaming video companies. They also must address issues that arise as governments work to regulate the internet. One of the biggest concerns for the streaming companies is **net neutrality**. This idea says that, online, consumers should have equal access to all the content available to them, without paying extra to an ISP to access a particular site. The ISPs cannot favor the content of one company over another. Defenders of net neutrality see the concept as part of the basic appeal of the internet.

Net neutrality was the standard for many years, though Congress failed several times to make it the law of the land. The Federal Communications Commission (FCC) also regulates TV and radio broadcasts and the internet. In 2015, it officially supported net neutrality. But the election of Donald Trump in 2016 led to rule changes. Under President Trump, the FCC was willing to give ISPs more power to limit access to certain content or make customers pay more for it. Netflix, Amazon, and other large internet companies opposed the end of net neutrality. In late 2017, the FCC approved a new plan that would do away with net neutrality rules. How this will affect consumers will be something to watch in the coming years.

Another issue the streaming companies face is taxes. Over the last few years, some states and cities have passed taxes on streaming video services. As people get rid of cable TV and buy fewer

It's entirely possible you will never pay for cable TV in your life.

DVDs, the states and cities lose tax money they once collected on those purchases. They want to make up for the loss of money by charging a tax on Netflix and other streaming services. The streaming companies oppose the taxes, since it means their customers have to pay more for the service. Some opponents of the taxes have gone to court to stop them from taking effect. In some cases, the opponents argue that the taxes on streaming services violate the Permanent Internet Tax Freedom Act. The law says states and cities cannot pass taxes that effect customers' access to the internet.

The different streaming companies also face pressures from within their own industry. The big four of Netflix, Amazon, Hulu, and Vudu have seen new and successful companies enter the field, such as Apple, Google (through YouTube, which it owns), and HBO. Even the social media company Twitter was entering the field. It reached agreements with Major League Baseball and several other professional sports organizations to stream live events. And at least one streaming company found success with a very narrow selection of content. Twitch live-streamed the best video gamers at play, and other video gamers were willing to pay to watch. Other content was available on demand.

With all this competition, the companies might find it hard to attract new customers. Netflix has continued to rely on foreign countries for its growth. By 2017, it had almost 100 million users, and almost half of them were overseas. Media experts thought that Hulu received a boost that year with the success of its original show *The Handmaid's Tale* at the Emmy Awards. The company planned to spend $2.5 billion on original programming in 2017. But that figure was still much less than the $5.8 billion Netflix was going to spend. Amazon came in between the two, at $4.5 billion.

There's no question that people around the world like the freedom streaming video gives them. A 2016 report predicted that by 2020, 80 percent of all the data moving through the internet would be for video. Much of that will be from people watching video on their smartphones and other mobile devices. In some cases, some experts believe, viewers might not choose just one streaming company over another. They might subscribe to several to get the original content each offers. The real losers could be the cable companies, as more people choose to cut the cord.

The Handmaid's Tale's **Emmy wins proved the worth of streaming services.**

In the years to come, watching streaming video will be an even bigger part of many people's lives. The best and biggest of the streaming companies will work even harder to keep those viewers happy.

Text-Dependent Questions

1. How has picture quality improved on TV and computer screens over the years since 1998?

2. What is one benefit of TVs that can show images in high dynamic range?

3. Why do Netflix and other content providers oppose taxes on streaming video services?

Research Project

Net neutrality is an ongoing issue between the FCC and internet companies. Go online to find an article from the last year or less that addresses net neutrality. Summarize the points it makes for and against net neutrality.

Find Out More

Books

Kallen, Stuart A. *Cutting Edge Entertainment Technology.* San Diego: ReferencePoint Press, 2017.

Mooney, Carla. *Music and Video Streaming.* New York: Rosen Publishing Group, 2016.

Sutherland, Adam. *Amazon: The Business Behind the "Everything" Store.* Minneapolis: Lerner Publications, 2016.

Websites

Broadband Speed Test

http://beta.speedtest.net/

How Streaming Video and Audio Work

http://computer.howstuffworks.com/internet/basics/streaming-video-and-audio.htm

Netflix

https://www.netflix.com/

Amazon Prime Video

https://www.amazon.com/Prime-Video/b?node=2676882011

Hulu

https://www.hulu.com

Vudu

https://www.vudu.com/

Series Glossary of Key Terms

algorithm   a set of steps a computer program follows to solve a problem or perform a certain task

bandwidth   a measurement of the data transferred from a website to the site's visitor

beta test   the public test of a computer product before its official release

bundle   the variety of TV channels available from a cable or streaming video company

broadband   the fastest internet connection available to most homes, usually offered through a cable TV service

cloud storage   a type of computer data storage where data is kept in remote servers and accessed through the internet

decoder   a program that translates data signals to make them visible on your computer

embed   in computing, to place a video or other piece of data within a web page or document

entrepreneurial   describing someone who develops and manages a business

firmware   software programming that is permanently part of a device

pixels   tiny dots on a TV or computer screen that form visible images

render   in computer graphics, the process of creating realistic images on screen using qualities such as lighting, shade, and perspective

stabilization   the ability of a product to hold a fixed position regardless of movement, shaking, or vibration

venture capitalists   people who give money to new companies, expecting to make more money in the future

Index

4K, 50-52, 55
actors, 41
ads, 22, 24, 26
algorithms, 14, 49
Alpha House, 37-38
Amazon, 8, 22-23, 25, 33-34, 39, 41-43, 51, 58-60
Amazon Prime, 35-36, 49
Amazon shows, 37-38, 40, 44
Apple, 17, 25, 27, 30-31, 34-35, 59
bandwidth, 11, 16, 51, 53, 55
Beasts of No Nation, 40, 56
Bezos, Jeff, 23, 33
binge-watching, 18, 38
cable TV, 7, 17, 43, 58
Comcast, 53
Disney, 23-24, 39, 43
DVDs, 11, 13, 18, 21, 29-31, 59
e-commerce, 33
Emmy Awards, 38-39, 44, 59
engineers, 11, 28, 49, 55
ESPN, 12
FCC, 57-58

Fox, 21-22, 27
Google, 27, 59
Handmaid's Tale, The, 44, 59
Hastings, Reed, 13-14, 17-18
HBO, 59
HD, 50-51
House of Cards, 38, 44
Hulu, 8, 21-23, 27, 29-30, 43-44, 51, 56, 59
Hulu Plus, 24, 26
Instant Video streaming, 37
ISPs, 53, 57-58
iTunes, 30-31
iTV, 17
kid TV shows, 39
Kilar, Jason, 22-24, 26
Lillyhammer, 37
Maranz, Tony, 27-29
Microsoft, 12
NCAA basketball, 52, 54
net neutrality, 57-59
Netflix, 8-9
    feature films, 41-42

shows, 37-38, 40, 55-56
subscribers, 15-16, 19, 25, 49
video quality, 49, 51-52
Oculus, 52
RealNetworks, 12
Roku, 25, 51
Rossmann, Alain, 27-28, 35
Silicon Valley, 27-28
Sony, 43, 50
Stranger Things, 55-56
Transparent, 44
Trudeau, Garry, 37
Turner Sports, 52, 54
TV networks, 21-24, 26-27, 36, 43-44, 50
Ultra HD, 50
Unbox, 33-35
venture capitalists, 28
video game devices, 34
Virtual Reality (VR), 52, 54-56
Visbit, 55
Vudu, 27-30, 43, 59
YouTube, 21, 56, 59

Picture Credits

A123RF: Hongee 17. Amazon: 36, 37. AP Images: Kyodo 23. Dreamstime.com: Goodluz 6; Arne9001 8; Gabriel Nardelli Araujo 10; Brandon Alms 15; Nmedia 16; Jovani Carlo Gorospe 30, 34; Josef Kubes 32; Tyler O'Neill 45; Louis Horch 46; Robert Kneschke 48; Semisatch 51; Andreaobzerova 52; Eimantas Buzas 53; Felix Miezioznikov 54. Newscom: Luci S. Huston/KRT 27; Albin Lohr-Jones/DPA/Picture-Alliance 35; Kento Nara/Geisler-Fotopress/Picture-Alliance 41; Kevin Dietsch/UPI 56; Christine Chew/UPI 60. Shutterstock: catwalker 13; ibreakstock 20; Mark Van Sycoc 22; DFree 24; DCWcreations 25; CasimiroPT 26; FeatureFlash 38; Kathy Hutchins 42; Zimmytws 58. Wikimedia CC: SounderBruce 12.

About the Author

Michael Burgan has written more than 250 books for children and teens, as well as newspaper articles and blog posts. Although not an athlete, he has written on both amateur and professional sports, including books on the Basketball Hall of Fame, the Olympics, and great moments in baseball. And although not a medical professional, he regularly writes web-content on a variety of health topics. He lives in Santa Fe, New Mexico, with his cat Callie.